I AM
WITH
YOU

I AM WITH YOU

LESSONS OF HOPE & COURAGE
in Times of Crisis

CARDINAL
TIMOTHY M. DOLAN

LOYOLA PRESS.
A JESUIT MINISTRY
Chicago

Other Books by Cardinal Timothy M. Dolan

Called to Be Holy

Doers of the Word

Who Do You Say I Am?

LOYOLA PRESS.
A JESUIT MINISTRY

3441 N. Ashland Avenue
Chicago, Illinois 60657
(800) 621-1008
www.loyolapress.com

Cover art credit: Pobytov/Digital Vision Vectors/Getty Images, Kotkoa/iStock/
Getty Images, Pinghung Chen/EyeEm/Getty Images, Eliks/Shutterstock.com.

ISBN: 978-0-8294-5415-4
Library of Congress Control Number: 2020948515

Printed in the United States of America.
20 21 22 23 24 25 26 27 28 29 30 Versa 10 9 8 7 6 5 4 3 2 1

This book is dedicated:
To all those who were sick with the coronavirus
and have now recovered, and to the loving memory
of those who died as a result of the disease. May
their souls, through the mercy of God, rest in peace;
To the heroic first responders of the
COVID-19 pandemic;
To the priests and deacons, men and women
religious, and all those who met the spiritual needs
of a people in crisis;
To the doctors, nurses, other healthcare
professionals, and caregivers who met the physical
needs of the sick and suffering, as well as family,
friends, and neighbors;
To the police officers, firefighters, and EMS workers
who responded to emergency calls at the risk of their
own health and safety;
And to all the other essential workers who kept our
towns, cities, states, and nation working.
May God bless you all!

Contents

Preface by
Cardinal Timothy M. Dolan

"I am with you always."
—Matthew 28:20

It sometimes takes a crisis for us to rediscover the clout of God's Holy Word. That's what happened to me the Sunday after Easter 2020, when that famous Gospel of "doubting Thomas" was read at Mass.

"Even though the doors were locked" (John 20:19), Jesus appeared to His disciples. This is awesome for two reasons: one, Jesus had just been brutally executed on the cross the Friday before, dead for sure. And now, here He is, alive, with us. Two, *the doors to the room where the disciples huddled were locked tight.* This cannot be understated. *How did Jesus get in?*

Why were those doors locked? Because those friends of the Lord were scared out of their wits, that's why. Those bully Roman soldiers who had tortured and executed their Lord were still on the prowl, as were other powerful folks who had sentenced Jesus to death.

Yet, "even though the doors were locked," Jesus showed up; He was there! Doubt no longer but believe!

Neither fear, adversity, tragedy, nor death can keep Jesus from being with us, His people. None of the powers on earth or under the earth can keep the Lord away from us, hard as they may try.

And they sure have tried hard in COVID-19. Fear and death were all around us. Unfortunately, they still linger.

We have been "behind locked doors" in quarantine, and many of us have been tempted to ask, "Where are you, Lord?"

While the Lord did not cause the pandemic, He can bring good from it as He brought life from death that first Easter.

Jesus has revealed to us that He is always with us, most powerfully when we're so scared, sad, anxious, and alone that we might ask if *He's* the one in quarantine. Where is He?

I am with you always.

What we've learned is that the locked doors of our doubts and trepidations cannot keep Jesus out.

I am grateful that so many of you kindly let me know that you appreciated my sermons from "America's Parish Church," St. Patrick's Cathedral, and some of my articles during the COVID-19 lockdown. Here they are, with some adjustments, in written form. I offer the words in this book to you for many reasons, but here are three. One, to capture a moment in time—in history—when all of us, including our holy Church, were challenged in ways many of us never expected. Two, to help us look back on this time and sense where God was present during the pandemic. And three, to help us to look forward by reminding all of us that whatever we are facing in life, whether it is illness, grief, job loss, isolation, anxiety, or the death of a loved one, Jesus is always with us.

Always.

As one of you touchingly wrote, "We were behind locked doors, yet Our Lord still came to be with us in so many ways!"

Amen. And God bless you.

† Timothy Michael Cardinal Dolan
Feast of the Holy Name of Jesus
January 3, 2021

CHAPTER 1

Living Water

Jesus answered and said to her,
"If you knew the gift of God
and who is saying to you, 'Give me a drink,'
you would have asked him
and he would have given you living water."

—John 4:10

It's eerie to see St. Patrick's Cathedral empty. We're used to seeing it jam-packed for Sunday Mass. Coming together in fellowship is an essential part of our Catholic life. Not being together is difficult.

Yet, even more important than the place where we worship is that we worship "in Spirit and in truth." As Our Lord says, "But the hour is coming, and is now here, when true worshipers will worship the Father in Spirit and truth" (John 4:23).

This, of course, is supreme at every Sunday Mass. And as much as we might miss Sunday Mass, we can still worship God in spirit and in truth.

We miss you. I hope you miss us. But one person who is never missing is God. And the Lord is particularly present with us at this tough time. There's a touching sense of unity, solidarity, and connectedness as we all feel particularly vulnerable and look to God our Father to take care of us. We trust that He does.

Our prayers during this time are particularly vigorous for those who are suffering, for those who have died, and for their families; for the physicians, nurses, emergency workers, and nursing home attendants, who work selflessly and sacrificially for our people who are homebound and apprehensive and fearful.

It is important to remember that regardless of what is happening in our lives, we always have the consoling words of Jesus to help and guide us. In particular there is much to learn, especially on how to pray, in the story of the Samaritan woman at the well. And I think you'd agree with me that we are always looking for a way to improve our prayers, especially during this tough time of COVID-19.

What this particular Scripture shows us is that there is an encounter between Jesus and the Samaritan woman. This, by its very nature, is what prayer is: a conversation with the Lord, a meeting and encounter with Jesus.

So, what other lessons might Jesus be teaching us? I have seven.

1. "So, he came to a town of Samaria called Sychar, near the plot of land that Jacob had given to his son Joseph. Jacob's well was there. Jesus, tired from his journey, sat down there at the well. It was about noon" (John 4:5–6). As this story opens, we see that Jesus makes the first move. He's there in the hot noon sun when this Samaritan woman comes to the well. She doesn't address Him; in fact, she ignores Him. But He's the one who initiates the conversation. This is an important lesson. More often than not, we think that we're doing God a big favor by praying to Him. But remember, it's always God's spark that initiates the conversation. It's always the Lord's prerogative. Yes, we do have a responsibility to pray, but we couldn't fulfill that if it wasn't for His grace and invitation. So even our ability to pray is a gift from

Him. He's the one who starts it as He did with the woman at the well.

2. "Give me a drink" (John 4:7). Jesus asks the woman for something. This is strange, because most of the time we approach prayer as us asking God for something. But here we have Jesus beginning the conversation by asking the woman for something. We know that this has always been interpreted as Him asking for the woman's faith. He's almost saying, "I thirst" as He will from the cross. It's as if He's saying, "I'm thirsting for your faith." I don't know if you've ever been to one of the convents of the Missionaries of Charity, Mother Teresa's sisters, but in every one of them, on the chapel wall below the cross, are these words: "I Thirst." Mother Teresa is saying that Jesus thirsts for our faith and our trust as He did with the woman in the gospel.

3. "[W]hoever drinks the water I shall give will never thirst" (John 4:14). In this conversation, Jesus reveals Himself to the woman as the living water. Usually, in prayer, God reveals something to us. He tells us about Himself and reminds us of His grace, love, mercy, and promises for us. When we priests pray our Divine Office, always on Sunday

morning, the psalm is "like the deer runs for living water, so my soul thirsts for you." Jesus came to quench that thirst. He is the living water that can quench the thirst of every human heart.

4. "Sir, please give me this water" (John 4:15). Notice that this is the start of the woman's conversion. She is admitting that she needs something she can't provide herself, that only Jesus can give. She is being humble. If we don't have humility in our prayer, we don't have much. In prayer, we can say, "I need something I can't give myself. I have a thirst that I cannot quench." That's humility.

5. The woman exhibits repentance. She knows in the face of her Savior that she's a sinner and needs the Lord's mercy.

6. "I'm the Messiah" (John 4:26). Jesus tells the woman who he is. This doesn't happen very often in the Gospels. We know by faith that He is the Messiah, but rarely does he speak so bluntly. But He does to this humble, repentant Samaritan woman.

7. "I have found the Messiah" (John 4:29). The Samaritan woman goes back to her village to tell the good news. She becomes a missionary, an

evangelist. The result of our conversation in prayer is missional, apostolic, and evangelical. We're so grateful for the gift of our faith, the living water that Jesus gives us. We want to leave our prayer and go tell others about it. We hope those others eventually come to believe, and, as the Gospel concludes, they ask, "Will you stay with us?" (John 4:40). And He says He will, and they'll have a conversation the next time they pray.

We pray more during this lockdown. This Gospel helps us do so!

Sunday Mass, March 15, 2020

READINGS FOR REFLECTION:
Exodus 17:3–7; Psalm 95:1–2, 6–7, 8–9; Romans 5:1–2, 5–8;
John 4:5–42

CHAPTER 2

The Infinite Sacrifice

I hope in the LORD, I trust in his word;
with him there is kindness and plenteous redemption.

—Psalm 130:5, 7

While it is true that no public Masses are being celebrated within our beloved Archdiocese of New York, it is also true that the Mass continues to be offered—we priests continue to pray with and for you, our beloved people, especially in this moment of worry and concern.

We are consoled by the truth of our Catholic faith: the greatest of all prayers, the Holy Sacrifice of the Mass, is so awesome that it goes beyond space and time. Anywhere we are—at home, on the road, in a hospital bed, or in those happy days when we could gather at our parishes in person—we can still unite ourselves to the Mass. It is the infinite, eternal sacrifice of praise, atonement, supplication, thanksgiving, and petition—the infinite sacrifice of the Son of God on the cross.

The Mass always continues. Always and everywhere. With an act of faith, we are absorbed into that magnificent prayer of Jesus on His cross that is renewed at every Mass.

Monday Mass, March 16, 2020

READINGS FOR REFLECTION:
2 Kings 5:1–15; Psalms 42:2–3; 43:3–4; Luke 4:24–30

CHAPTER 3

Share the Faith

*Therefore, I teach you the statutes and decrees
as the LORD, my God, has commanded me,
that you may observe them in the land
you are entering to occupy.*

—Deuteronomy 4:5

In the Book of Deuteronomy, Moses says, "However, be on your guard and be very careful not to forget the things your own eyes have seen, nor let them slip from your heart as long as you live, but make them known to your children and to your children's children" (4:9). Moses is encouraging the people of Israel to take to heart the teachings and instructions of God and pass them on to their children and grandchildren.

Yesterday, I was talking to a gentleman who had been sick for some time. He's recovered now, praise God. He said to me, "I'm having a good time. I've been living at my daughter's house, and I'm babysitting for three of my grandkids who are all home from school. *I'm actually homeschooling them.* They enjoy it, and I love it. We go from eight to noon, and the kids know that if they're good and learn their lessons well, they're going to get a hot fudge sundae."

I asked what he's teaching them. He said they do some geography, some science, and some math. And I said, "How about teaching your grandkids the rosary?" He said he hadn't thought of that, but he agreed it was a good idea.

I could see the excitement in his eyes, so I asked him, "How did you learn to pray the rosary?" And he said, "Well, come to think of it, my grandparents taught it to me."

Teaching others to pray is a beautiful and simple example of doing what Moses said: pass on the faith, pass on our prayers, pass on the teachings of the Lord to our children and grandchildren.

We give the sharing of faith a fancy name in the Church: *tradition*, which comes from the Latin word *traditio*, "to hand over, to give to another for safekeeping." In the Church we are called to hand over the faith to others. God the Father depended on His Only Begotten Son to teach us about the faith. And what did Jesus do? He handed His teaching over to His apostles, who then handed it over to generation after generation. That's how we received it, and it's our job to keep the tradition going.

These days, many of us find ourselves saying, "What am I going to do today? Everything is closed." Those of us who have the opportunity to hand on the faith, like that grandpa with whom I spoke, can see this as a providential time to do so.

Wednesday Mass, March 18, 2020

READINGS FOR REFLECTION:
Deuteronomy 4:1, 5–9; Psalm 147:12–13, 15–16, 19–20;
Matthew 5:17–19

CHAPTER 4

I Do Believe, Lord

As Jesus passed by he saw a man blind from birth.
His disciples asked him,
"Rabbi, who sinned, this man or his parents,
that he was born blind?"
Jesus answered,
"Neither he nor his parents sinned;
it is so that the works of God might be
made visible through him."

—John 9:1–3

In the Gospel of John, Jesus, the great teacher that He is, cures a man born blind of his physical blindness. Jesus is also telling us that we are all spiritually blind. We are all born into darkness, and Jesus alone is the light of the world that can cure that darkness. So, keep that major theme in mind as I mention three lessons that I hope can help us appreciate this Gospel a bit more.

1. "Rabbi, who sinned, this man or his parents, that he was born blind?" (John 9:2). Jesus' disciples ask a good, logical question. Don't we all, at times, ask the reason for evil and sorrow in this world? It's a good question to ask. In fact, we're all asking the question now: Why this coronavirus? Why is there evil? Where does it come from?

Sometimes we can cite a cause for evil. I know when I visit a prison and speak with the prisoners, obviously they're suffering incarceration. But they typically know the reason for that. They'll say, "I know the reason for this incarceration, and I deserve it. I committed a crime, and here I am." They know the reason they're in prison.

And sometimes I'll visit someone in the hospital who's dying from lung cancer, and they'll say, "I know the reason for this. I smoked two packs of cigarettes a day my entire adult life." These people realize the effects of their actions. They know the reason for this disease.

But these are kind of rare instances, aren't they? Most of the time we don't know the answer to the question of evil, or of suffering and sickness. And so, we're glad when Jesus is asked, "Lord, why is this man blind? Is it his sin or his parents' sin?" Because it means he's going to give us an answer.

We do get an answer. Maybe not the one we were expecting, but he responds to us nonetheless. Jesus tells us what the cause of the suffering is *not*: "Neither he nor his parents sinned; it is so that the works of God might be made visible through him" (John 9:3). I'm glad He said that. I'd have a tough time believing in a tender, loving, caring Father who punishes His children with strange diseases and tragedies like this man born blind. I find Jesus' words consoling. He says this man was born blind so that God's work can be visible through him. In other words, through his own blindness and suffering, and, as we find out, through his healing, God's work and God's light will be shown. So what Jesus is teaching us is that His light and healing can come through tragedies if we trust in Him.

Many of us are asking the *why* of the coronavirus. We know it's not due to punishment for our sins. Of course, some people think it is. You just have to look at the internet for that. But one thing we believers learn is instead of asking *why*, which we can't really answer, we ought to ask *who*. Who can bring meaning during times of crisis? Who can bring resolution to our problems and fears? Who can give us purpose? And that, of course, is Almighty God.

2. Do you notice how Jesus cures the man born blind? He could have just snapped His fingers and said, "Regain your sight." But instead Jesus takes His time. He bends over, spits on the ground, and makes clay with His saliva. He applies it gingerly to the man's eyes, rubbing the salve on them, and then He says, "Go wash in the Pool of Siloam." The blind man does, and his sight is restored. He can see.

Just as Jesus used water, ointment, touch, and words to heal the man, so does His Church heal us in the seven sacraments. In the Sacrament of Baptism, we use water, like the blind man did in the Pool of Siloam. We also use the oil of catechumens and the oil of chrism to anoint the baby or adult, like Jesus did with the clay. We use the oil of chrism in the Sacrament of Confirmation as well as the imposition of hands at the Sacrament of Holy Orders. We use the oil of the sick when we anoint the infirm. We use words of consent in the Sacrament of Matrimony and at the Sacrament of Penance.

That's why this is a tough time for the Church. Like Jesus, His Church is tactile and hands-on. The sacraments—bread and wine, oil and water, words of consent and the imposition of hands—cannot be done at a distance. This is the power of healing that the sacraments offer. Through them we can achieve spiritual illumination. They open our eyes as Jesus opened the eyes of the man born blind.

Throughout the country and the archdiocese, we hear God's people say, "We miss the sacraments. We want Mass, Holy Communion, Confession, Anointing of the Sick, Confirmation, Baptism, Matrimony, and Holy Orders. We need the Gospels. We believe that Jesus heals and works through these seven ancient, powerful signs."

Thanks be to God, our bishops and priests and deacons are trying their best in extraordinary circumstances to see that God's people, especially those who are sick and suffering, have access to the sacraments. I'm as eager as you are to see the visible sacramental life of the Church restored as soon as possible. Yet this is a special opportunity to make an act of faith in the power of the sacraments. During Mass and throughout the day, say to yourself, "Jesus, we believe you still work in and through your Church, in your sacraments."

3. The man born blind grows in his appreciation and understanding of who Jesus is. At first, his neighbors asked him how his eyes were opened, and he said, "The man called Jesus made clay and anointed my eyes and told me, 'Go to Siloam and wash'" (John 9:11).

A little later, the Pharisees asked him how he's able to see, and the blind man says, "He is a prophet" (John 9:17).

And finally, after the man is thrown out by the Pharisees, Jesus finds him and asks him, "Do you believe in the Son of Man?" The man replies, "Who is he?" Jesus answers, "The one speaking to you right now is He." And the blind man says, "I do believe, Lord" and worships him (John 9:38).

You only worship the divine. So, from "the man" to a prophet to the Son of God, the blind man grows in his understanding of who Jesus is. So do we. The gift of faith is implanted within us on the day of our baptism. But sometimes it takes a while for that to develop. One of the ways it does develop is in a time of crisis. This is a time when I hear many people with whom I speak say they're turning to Jesus more. They're turning to God. Their prayers have been dormant, and they have cared only about themselves, but now they find themselves feeling hopeless and alone. They're turning to Jesus as their Lord and Savior. Their faith is developing and maturing in a difficult time, like it did for that man born blind.

Jesus is the light of the world who can cure the darkness that afflicts us all. I'm finding myself welcoming light these days. Yesterday, in spite of it all, when I took a little walk outside, it was bright. The sun was out even at six in the evening. The first day of spring was just the other day, and the light was so refreshing, pushing back the wintry, chilling, morbid darkness. It reminds us that Jesus is the light of the world.

I'm sure you know a line from a popular song from the musical *Mame*, "We need a little Christmas right this very minute." Let me change it a little bit: we need a little Easter right this very minute. That's when the light of Easter Sunday morning definitively conquers the darkness of Good Friday afternoon.

Sunday Mass, March 22, 2020

READINGS FOR REFLECTION:
Hosea 6:1–6; Psalm 51:3–4, 18–19, 20–21; Luke 18:9–14

CHAPTER 5

Imagine

See, I am creating new heavens
and a new earth;
The former things shall not be remembered
nor come to mind.
Instead, shout for joy and be glad forever
in what I am creating.

—Isaiah 65:17–18

Recently, a group of musicians and singers reinterpreted John Lennon's song "Imagine." They tried to apply it to the difficulties and adversities we're going through today with the coronavirus. What they're saying is, imagine there is no sickness. Imagine there is no fever. Imagine there is no death. No tears. No sorrow.

As a Christian, I know that there are many problematic parts of John Lennon's original song, but the Lord composed a song without those problematic parts. It can be found in the Book of Isaiah:

"Thus says the Lord: Lo, I am about to create new heavens and a new earth . . . /No longer shall the sound of weeping be heard there, /or the sound of crying; /no longer shall there be in it an infant who lives but a few days, /or an old man who does not round out his full lifetime." (Isaiah 65:17–20)

Isaiah is inviting us to imagine a new heaven and a new earth. To imagine, people who die at 100 to be thought of as dying early! Isaiah asks us to imagine no sickness, no war, no tears. That, of course, is God's design for us. It was His intention at the beginning of all creation, in the Garden of Eden. His original intention was original happiness, which we sadly turned into Original Sin.

God's design was to live in harmony with His people, where all our needs would be taken care of, and we would have happiness because we would be close to God and in accordance with His will.

But Satan, and the misuse of our own free will that God has given us, distorted all that. And so, we have the crumbling, the fracturing, the division, the sorrow, the sadness, the sickness, and the death that we know today.

And yet, God still challenges us to imagine. His Son will return to judge the living and the dead, to usher in a new heaven and a new earth—His Second Coming. We can imagine that. We long for that. We hope for that, especially now as we're going through difficulties. We imagine, we pray, we trust, we hope, we have faith that God will set everything right.

He told us He would.

Monday Mass, March 23, 2020

READINGS FOR REFLECTION:
1 Samuel 16:1b, 6–7, 10–13a; Psalm 23:1–3a, 3b–4, 5, 6;
Ephesians 5:8–14; John 9:1–41

CHAPTER 6

Be Not Afraid

God is our refuge and our strength,
an ever-present help in distress.
Therefore we fear not, though the earth be shaken
and mountains plunge into the depths of the sea.

—Psalm 46:2–3

Crises help us recover the basics we have ignored. In Catholic life, what is most essential is Jesus, our faith and trust in Him. Another basic belief is that one of the most powerful ways that Jesus remains with us is in the Holy Eucharist—Mass and Holy Communion.

In recent decades, researchers have reported that our faith in the sacraments and our participation at Sunday Mass have gone down. Most of us don't need researchers to tell us this. We can see these changes through observation.

Our current trauma, the onslaught of the coronavirus, has caused suffering and struggle for so many of us: those affected by it for sure, but also their families, our elders and homebound, our brave medical professionals, our civic leaders, those now in financial anxiety, our kids who are out of school and the parents who care for them, and so many who are scared.

The Bible, and history, tell us that in times of plague (now), war, famine, natural disaster, and economic woe, people turn to interior strength, to one another, and to the Lord!

A faith that may have been dormant or ignored is rediscovered, a trust in the Lord who repeated over and over again, "Be not afraid," and in a Savior who taught, "Fear is useless. What is needed is trust."

For us as Catholics, a recovered faith means cherishing anew the sacraments.

Understandably, from the Bishop of Rome, Pope Francis, down to the Bishop of New York, yours truly, tough decisions have been made to halt temporarily the public celebration of the Mass and the sacraments, as we take seriously our high moral obligation to protect the health of our people.

As necessary as this is, we bishops, priests, deacons, pastoral leaders, and our people are longing for the return of the Mass and the sacraments. We need them! We want them!

Thank God at least that our churches are open for prayer, that the Mass is available to us on radio, TV, and livestream, that our priests are "on duty" and available in careful, safe ways for the Sacraments of Penance, Anointing of the Sick, Baptism, Matrimony, and funerals in small, private, and controlled situations.

Not the same, though, is it? We all realize that.

With Holy Week, Easter, Confirmations, First Holy Communions, weddings, ordinations, religious professions, and anniversaries on the horizon, we are especially eager for the communal life of the Church through worship and the sacraments to kick back in. We're poised to do that the moment we're advised it's safe.

For now, though, we can rejoice in the swelling chorus of people chanting throughout the planet, "We want Mass! We need the sacraments! We love them! We miss them!"

How refreshing!

Wednesday Mass, March 25, 2020

READINGS FOR REFLECTION:
Ezekiel 47:1–9, 12; Psalm 46:2–3, 5–6, 8–9; John 5:1–16

CHAPTER 7

And Jesus Wept

So the sisters sent word to him saying,
"Master, the one you love is ill."
When Jesus heard this he said,
"This illness is not to end in death,
but is for the glory of God,
that the Son of God may be glorified through it."

—John 11:3–4

In chapter 11 of John's Gospel, we read about Jesus raising His friend Lazarus from the dead. It's a beautiful and meaty Gospel. If we look closely, we find that there are some veiled messages for us as well. Let me point out seven messages that might go unnoticed.

1. Jesus had good friends: Martha, Mary, and Lazarus. He loved them, and he relished their hospitality. He would visit them often, as the village where they lived was only an hour or so

walk from Jerusalem. Why did the Son of God need friends? Because this Gospel teaches us a timeless truth of our Catholic faith—yes, He's true God, but He's also true man, and like any human being He needed friends.

2. When these good friends were in need, they called on their friend, Jesus. Lazarus was ill, and so the sisters sent word to Him, saying, "Master, the one you love is ill" (John 11:3). The Gospel goes on to say, "Now Jesus loved Martha and her sister and Lazarus" (John 11:5). As we read these consoling words, it's good for us to remember that Jesus is our friend. He's the only begotten Son of God, but He's also our best friend. He loves us and we love Him.

As we see in John 15:15, the Lord says, "I no longer call you slaves, because a slave does not know what his master is doing. I have called you friends." We, like Martha and Mary, need friends during this trauma that our city, state, and nation are going through. And like Martha and Mary, we call Jesus to be our friend in this time of trial and adversity. Jesus is with us. He's always near. There's no quarantine or lockdown that can keep

Him away from us. We may have a difficult time believing that.

In fact, when Jesus arrives in Bethany, Martha says, "Lord, if you had been here, my brother would not have died" (John 11:21). Sometimes when we call on our friend Jesus, we ask, "Where were you? What took you so long?" But this Gospel teaches us that Jesus, our friend, is indeed with us at every moment.

As we see in Matthew 28:20, the Lord says, "I am with you always, until the end of the age." Jesus, our friend, our Savior, and our Divine Physician, is with us through others. I think of our brave physicians, nurses, and healthcare workers. I think of family and friends at home who are caring for the sick. I think of people in our Catholic Charities, and so many agencies throughout the country, that are coming through with the presence of God, with the healing, consolation, and unity that the Lord gives us. They are all part of the friendship that Jesus gives us.

3. When the messenger tells Jesus that Lazarus is sick, Jesus says, "This illness is not to end in death, but is for the glory of God, that the Son of God may be glorified through it" (John 11:4). Jesus

can—and does—bring light from darkness, good from evil, healing from illness, life from death. We believe that Jesus can transform anything into the glory of God.

4. We must have faith. What a great example Martha and Mary are. Yes, they were a little irritated with Jesus and asked where He had been, but their faith triumphed. Because after Martha says that Lazarus would not have died had Jesus been there, she immediately says, "But even now I know that whatever you ask of God, God will give you" (John 11:22). That's faith. That's the faith we need, the faith of Martha and Mary.

5. "And Jesus wept" (John 11:35). He cried at the tomb of Lazarus. In just a moment, He's going to show us that He's true God as He raises Lazarus from the dead. But right now, He's showing us that we have a God who cries. We have a God whose Sacred Heart is broken. We can imagine that He's crying not just because of the sadness of Martha and Mary, not just because of the suffering and death of his friend Lazarus. He's crying because He knows that this is not the life His Father intended for us. When God created us, He didn't want sickness and death. He created a world

where there was none. And only because of the evil and sin that fractured His original goodness did these things come about. So even as we confront the turmoil and suffering and death, we cry. God cries. Because He didn't intend it. He didn't want it. When we cry because bad things happen, know that Jesus is crying with us, too.

6. Jesus raises Lazarus from the dead. This isn't the first time that Jesus raises someone from the dead. He raised the son of the widow of Nain. He raised the daughter of Jairus. He does it now for Lazarus, but here's the hidden meaning: Lazarus, the son of the widow of Nain, and the daughter of Jairus all came back from the dead. And yet they all died eventually. What Jesus is telling us is that He will raise all of us to life everlasting. He's telling us about the gift of eternal life that He came to bring us.

With the raising of Lazarus from the dead, He's saying, I want to do something greater. I want to give you the gift of everlasting life. That will come shortly after, through His saving death and glorious Resurrection.

This reminds me of a story. I was visiting somebody in the hospital a while back, and as I left him, the gentleman in the room next to him said, "Hey Reverend, can I see you for a moment?" I said sure. He said, "I'm not Catholic. I don't even have any religion. But I've just been told I'm going to die. I've got an incurable disease, and it's only a matter of time. Can you go out and help find me a second opinion?" I said I couldn't help him with that. He said, "Well, can you go out and look up some other medicine I can take?" I said I couldn't help him with that, either. And he began to cry and said, "But I want to live forever." And I said, "Well, that I can help you with. Will you let me tell you about Jesus, the Resurrection and the Life?"

7. When Lazarus shuffled out of the tomb—remember, he's bound up like a mummy in the burial cloths—Jesus says to the people, "Untie him and let him go" (John 11:44). Sometimes it's translated as "loose him" or "free him" or "liberate him." Lazarus was in the bondage of death, and Jesus says, "Untie him."

I was meeting with a young man who had battled terrible addictions: oxycodone and alcohol. After several years, he gained sobriety, sanity, and health. Whenever he'd see me, he'd always want to pray. Which is good; I love to pray all the time, too. When I suggested we take a passage from the Bible to help us in our prayer, he asked to use the eleventh chapter of the Gospel of John—the raising of Lazarus. He didn't read the whole passage. He went down to the point where Jesus called Lazarus out of the tomb and said, "Untie him." And the young man said, "I never forget those words. I was tied up. I was in bondage to death and everything that was leading to my death. And Jesus said to me as He did to Lazarus, 'Untie him. Leave the tomb. Get out of bondage. Come back to life.'" And the young man said, "Here I am." That's the most powerful interpretation of that passage I've ever heard.

All through life, we go through dying and rising. We're in a period of dying right now throughout the world from COVID-19. But we know that the rising will come.

Sunday Mass, March 29, 2020

READINGS FOR REFLECTION:
Ezekiel 37:12–14; Psalm 130:1–2, 3–4, 5–6, 7–8; Romans 8:8–11;
John 11:1–45

Chapter 8

Hosanna!

*The crowds preceding him and those following
kept crying out and saying:
"Hosanna to the Son of David;
blessed is he who comes in the name of the Lord;
hosanna in the highest."
And when he entered Jerusalem
the whole city was shaken and asked, "Who is this?"
And the crowds replied,
"This is Jesus the prophet, from Nazareth in Galilee."*

—Matthew 21:9–11

The two Sundays bookending Holy Week, Palm Sunday and Easter Sunday, are days of exultation and acclaim. On Palm Sunday, as Jesus enters Jerusalem, the crowds are crying out: "Hosanna to the Son of David; blessed is He who comes in the name of the lord; Hosanna in the highest" (Matthew 21:9). Then, on Easter Sunday, Jesus defeats sin and Satan, darkness, suffering, and death by His glorious Resurrection. The strife is over, and the battle won.

But we're somberly realistic as we acknowledge what's on the shelf between those two happy bookends: Jesus' betrayal, His gruesome Passion, His suffering and death on the cross. Long have we faithful contemplated the meaning of that dramatic decline in the fate of Jesus that occurred between Palm Sunday and Good Friday.

Think about what happened. The crowds on Palm Sunday, intrigued by his teaching and moved by His miracles—especially by His raising of Lazarus from the dead only a day or two before—were uplifted by His promises, enthralled by His invitation to follow Him, and wanted to be near Him whatever happened. Oh, from that good time on Palm Sunday to the horror, sadness, fear, hopelessness, darkness, and degradation of Good Friday afternoon; from the crowds shouting "Hosanna!" to the mob yelling "Crucify him!"; from friends claiming they'd never abandon Him, to those same ones running away when He needed them most; from Peter boasting, "I am prepared to go to prison and to die with you" (Luke 22:33) to the same Peter, a blubbering coward, telling a maid in the courtyard, "Woman, I do not know him" (Luke 22:57).

From the crowd waving palms to soldiers waving spears, jeering, and spitting on Him; from the shouts of "Son of David" to the taunts that no, he's a brigand, an enemy, considered a worm, not a man; from the throng expressing faith to the crowds mocking Him and demanding His death: those who had hoped now grow cynical, those who believed now doubt, those close to Him now run, and those who trusted in Him now scatter. Perhaps among those who shouted "Crucify him!" on Good Friday are those who acclaimed "Hosanna!" to Him on Palm Sunday.

We find ourselves now in a Good Friday moment. With this vicious coronavirus, we're apprehensive, anxious, and alone. Many people have been attacked by the virus, with family and friends worried and brave healthcare workers tending to them. I hate to say it, but we may be tempted to lose trust in the One we believe to be Our Lord, lured to doubt Him, even to abandon Him. We may be led to remain in this Good Friday moment of rejecting Him, mocking Him, believing that darkness, despair, and death have the last word instead of the Word, the One who is our life and our light: Jesus, my Lord, my God, my all.

This Palm Sunday we acclaim that we are not fair-weather friends of Jesus. We are faithful, not fickle.

We hope and do not holler "Away with him!" You know who said it far better than I ever could, centuries ago, is Thomas à Kempis, in his classic *The Imitation of Christ*:

"Jesus has always many who love His heavenly kingdom, but few who bear His cross. He has many who desire consolation, but few who care for trial. He finds many to share His table, but few to take part in His fasting. All desire to be happy with Him; few wish to suffer anything for Him. Many follow Him to the breaking of the bread, but few to the drinking of the chalice of His Passion. Many revere His miracles, few approach the shame of His cross. Many love Him as long as they encounter no hardship; many praise and bless Him as long as they receive some comfort from Him. But if Jesus seems to hide Himself and leaves them for a while, they fall either into complaints or into deep dejection. Those, on the contrary, who love Him for His own sake and not for any comfort of their own, bless Him in all trial and anguish of heart as well as in the bliss of consolation."

My brothers and sisters in Christ, our Holy Week journey might be stalled on Good Friday afternoon. But we never drop those palms of victory, for Easter is soon near. God is the beginning and the end, the starting line and the finish line. What comes in between can never separate us from the love of God.

Palm Sunday Mass, April 5, 2020

CHAPTER 9

Suffering Servant

The LORD called me from birth,
from my mother's womb he gave me my name.
He made of me a sharp-edged sword
and concealed me in the shadow of his arm.

—Isaiah 49:1–2

In the Book of Isaiah, we read of the "Suffering Servant." In these writings, we anticipate Jesus, the supreme Suffering Servant: "For now the Lord has spoken who formed me as his servant from the womb" (Isaiah 49:5).

It's a magnificent reflection on God's providence. God has a plan and a design. History is *His story,* the unfolding of the way He intends it.

The Suffering Servant knew that. Jesus knew that. We need to acknowledge that again today. When we see the difficulties, tragedies, and trauma in the world today because of the coronavirus, many of us wonder, Does God know what He's doing?

God always knows what He's doing. We sometimes can't figure it out. But as St. Paul would say, "We know that all things work for good for those who love God, who are called according to his purpose" (Romans 8:28).

Tuesday Mass, April 7, 2020

READINGS FOR REFLECTION:
Isaiah 49:1–6; Psalm 71:1–2, 3–4a, 5ab–6ab, 15–17;
John 13:21–33, 36–38

CHAPTER 10

Do This in Memory of Me

"You call me 'teacher' and 'master,' and rightly so,
for indeed I am.
If I, therefore, the master and teacher,
have washed your feet,
you ought to wash one another's feet.
I have given you a model to follow,
so that as I have done for you, you should also do."

—John 13:13–15

Jesus is at the center of every Mass, every liturgy, and every prayer. Our attention is riveted on Him, especially on Holy Thursday, Good Friday, the Easter Vigil, and the glorious Easter Sunday morning. So tonight, on Holy Thursday, we center ourselves on Jesus and the gifts He's given us on the night before he died: the gift of the Holy Eucharist, the gift of the Sacrament of Holy Orders, and the dramatic example of a servant washing the feet of His apostles.

Put yourself in the place of Jesus for a moment. He had every right in the world to be self-occupied, to feel sorry for Himself, to be self-absorbed in His anxiety over the horror that He knew awaited Him. Picture Jesus sweating drops of blood in the agony in the garden; the yawning of his supposed friends who fell asleep when He asked them for their company; the betrayal by one of His own, Judas Iscariot; seeing all of His apostles but one, John the Beloved Disciple, run off. And then to be tortured, scourged, crowned with thorns, taunted, unjustly condemned, spit upon, forced to carry His heavy cross to Calvary; nailed to those beams; heckled by soldiers; and, after three excruciating hours, to die on the cross. We could expect Jesus, only hours before at His Last Supper, to curl up, complain bitterly, think only of Himself, and shiver with fear and trepidation. What, instead, did He do?

He was not selfish, but selfless. As St. John, the only one of the Twelve not to abandon Him, recounts in the Gospel: "Jesus knew that His hour had come to pass from this world to the Father. He loved His own in the world and He loved them to the end" (John 13:1).

He took care of the apostles with three lavish gifts.

First, He gave them a stunning act of selfless sacrificial service. Even though he was the Messiah, he washed the feet of His apostles as if He were a slave. Second, He gave them the gift of the most Holy Eucharist, by which He feeds us and remains with us to this very moment, by changing bread and wine into His very Body and Blood. And third, He gave us the priesthood, to continue that gift of the Holy Eucharist, instructing them to "do this in memory of me."

We really need this example of Jesus right now. We're scared and anxious, discouraged by this pandemic all around us. We could be excused for curling up and feeling sorry for ourselves, being bitter if we are afflicted or worrying over someone close to us who is.

Or we could imitate Jesus, thinking not of ourselves but of others, loving them till the end. This solemn evening, on the night before He died, as we are inspired by the example of the Savior's selfless love, we can praise God for those who emulate Him: from those who take the temperatures and tend to the sick, to those who pick up garbage and drive our trains and buses; from those workers deemed essential, always at risk, to those who are burying our dead; from those who drop off meals, to those who fill prescriptions; from police and fire departments, hospital maintenance crews and first responders, to chaplains anointing the dying.

The self-giving example of Jesus on that first Holy Thursday goes on every day. The grace of His example of love and service overshadows the mighty temptation to selfishness.

Thank God for those who whisper with Jesus, "Not my will but yours be done" (Luke 22:42).

This selflessness of Jesus on Holy Thursday will lead to the pouring out of His life on the cross on Good Friday. We acknowledge that, but the selflessness doesn't stop there. It continues into Easter, as light dispels the darkness, as we savor the defeat of sin, Satan, death, and selfishness.

Holy Thursday, Mass of the Lord's Supper, April 9, 2020

READINGS FOR REFLECTION:
Isaiah 50:4–9a; Psalm 69:8–10, 21–22, 31, 33–34; Matthew 26:14–25

Chapter 11

He Is Not Here

Then the angel said to the women in reply,
"Do not be afraid!
I know that you are seeking Jesus the crucified.
He is not here, for he has been raised just as he said.
Come and see the place where he lay."

—Matthew 28:5–6

We miss a lot of people and things these tough days. We miss the company of family and friends due to the coronavirus. We miss going out, maybe to our favorite diner or coffee shop or tavern.

Those who have lost someone dear to them because of the pandemic miss them deeply. We miss just being near our loved ones who are in hospitals or care facilities. We miss our jobs. Kids miss school.

On this Easter Vigil, I miss our candidates and catechumens. Since last fall, here in the Archdiocese of New York and in our three hundred parishes, over a thousand people have been preparing to enter into full communion with the Church this holy night through the Sacraments of Baptism, Confirmation, and Holy Communion. They've studied and prayed under devoted catechists and sponsors for this grand evening. And we miss them.

You see, when Jesus rose from the dead that first Easter, he triumphed over sin and Satan and evil and death. But it was not just a personal victory for Him. While it was indeed that, He shares that triumph with all of us. We are invited to become part of His new risen life through the seven sacraments of the Church.

When we're baptized, He destroys the sin in our soul that we call Original Sin. He claims us for Himself and gives us the invitation to live forever with Him. He adopts us as a child of God and a member of our supernatural family, the Church.

When we receive Him in Holy Communion, He dwells within us. That life of Christ at Easter dwells in our souls. When we're confirmed, He strengthens that life and shares that dwelling in our souls with another person, the third Person of the Holy Trinity—God the Holy Spirit.

The sacraments are a powerful way that we participate in the victory of Jesus by His Resurrection.

That's why I miss our candidates and catechumens tonight, because their reception of the sacraments at parishes across the country shows us that the victory of Christ at Easter continues.

Many of you tell me that you, too, miss the sacraments, as our churches are unfortunately (but understandably) closed. You believe that through these sacraments, you, too, share in the light, life, healing, promises, and victory of Christ at Easter.

But one person whom we do not miss is Jesus, because He is here. He is with you right now, wherever you might be. He dwells in your very heart and soul. "I will not leave you orphans," He says to us in John 14:18. And again, in Matthew 28:20, the Lord tells us, "And behold, I am with you always, until the end of the age." That's how close Jesus is to all of us now.

Years ago, when I was a parish priest back in St. Louis, I got to know a young man who got in trouble and was sentenced to prison. Two years later, he completed his sentence and was released from prison. But he didn't have anybody to pick him up, so he asked if I would come get him. And I did. I'd gotten to know the guards rather well because I visited the prison frequently, and they let me help him clean out his cell. He had a cardboard box filled with the belongings that had been in his cell for those two years. As he was leaving, the guards said, "Anything else in there you want to take with you?" The freed man replied, "Well, Jesus was in there with me those two years. And even though He's coming with me, tell the next guy that gets confined to this cell that Jesus is still in there if he needs Him."

That man leaving jail understood the mystery of Easter: Jesus is with us, risen from the dead.

We're missing a lot these tough days, but we sure cannot miss Him.

Easter Vigil of the Lord's Resurrection, April 11, 2020

READINGS FOR REFLECTION:
Isaiah 52:13—53:12; Psalm 31:2, 6, 12–13, 15–16, 17, 25;
Hebrews 4:14–16; 5:7–9; John 18:1—19:42

CHAPTER 12

Empty

On the first day of the week,
Mary of Magdala came to the tomb
early in the morning,
while it was still dark,
and saw the stone removed from the tomb.
So she ran and went to Simon Peter
and to the other disciple whom Jesus loved,
and told them,
"They have taken the Lord from the tomb,
and we don't know where they put him."

—John 20:1–2

When the women arrived at the tomb, they found it empty. *Empty.*

I'll admit that talking about emptiness might sound somewhat contradictory on Easter Sunday. After all, Easter is about fullness. Easter is about light and triumph and hope and life. And here I am talking about emptiness?

But the Easter message starts with that empty tomb. The holy women, and then Peter and John, came to the tomb early that first Easter morning and found it empty. The Roman guard posted by Pontius Pilate had fled at something extraordinary. What had happened? An angel said to the women, "Why do you seek the living among the dead?" (Luke 24:5).

The emptiness of the tomb signifies that He had, indeed, risen from the dead. The dramatic, overwhelming emptiness of Good Friday afternoon—still fresh in memory, when the world was empty of hope and life itself—gives way to the empty tomb and the fullness of Easter glory.

During my senior year of high school, my dad told me that the old beat-up Plymouth station wagon was now mine to use to drive back and forth from school. I was thrilled. Of course, he said, "Now you need to take care of it. And it needs new oil." So I ran off to get some oil, came home, and asked my dad where to pour this new, fresh oil. His response was simple: "First, we have to empty the old, dirty stuff."

That lesson is pretty basic: emptiness before fullness.

My Jewish friends tell me that's why God led His people through the desert as described in the Book of Exodus. There were easier, more direct routes to get there, so why did the Lord choose the desert? Because it's barren and empty. The Jews would have to depend on the Lord to fulfill all their needs.

When you think about it, isn't that why we have Lent? We empty ourselves of sin and selfishness so He can fill us with His mercy and new life at Easter.

When we renew our baptismal promises, we empty ourselves of sin to be filled with His grace. That is the journey from the emptiness of Good Friday to the abundance of Easter Sunday, from the empty tomb to the risen Christ.

I bring all this up because we hear plenty about emptiness during these days of the dreaded pandemic.

There are empty dinner tables for Passover and Easter because family and friends can't get together; empty schools and factories; empty restaurants, roads, and airplanes; empty wallets and empty bank accounts; empty chairs at home where those we cherished used to sit with us; empty churches; empty lives.

On this paschal morning, I ask if the empty tomb of Easter is a metaphor for our world and our lives.

Could it be a whispered invitation from the Risen One to search for the Living One not among the dead?

As Alexander Solzhenitsyn, the towering Russian human-rights prophet from the last century, who spent many Easters in a gulag, wrote, "The worst oppression is a life without God."

Emptiness can be a blessing, not a curse. It is the God of the living who fills us with life, meaning, resolve, light, and hope. He has risen as He said he would. *Alleluia, Alleluia.*

"Union with Jesus," preaches Pope Francis, "risen and ever living, anticipates that Sunday without sunset. When there will be no more weariness nor pain. There will be no more sorrow nor tears. Instead, we will have only the joy of being fully and forever with our Risen Lord."

"And when they arrived at the tomb, they found it empty."

Easter Sunday Mass, April 12, 2020

READINGS FOR REFLECTION:
Acts of the Apostles 10:34a, 37–43; Psalm 118:1–2, 16–17, 22–23;
Colossians 3:1–4; John 20:1–9

CHAPTER 13

The Doors Were Locked

On the evening of that first day of the week,
when the doors were locked, where the disciples were,
for fear of the Jews,
Jesus came and stood in their midst
and said to them, "Peace be with you."

—John 20:19

On Divine Mercy Sunday, we always have the same Gospel reading, from the twentieth chapter of John. It's the famous episode where Jesus visits His disciples that first Easter Sunday evening. There's so much for inspiration in this passage. Here are three lessons for today:

1. "The doors were locked" (John 20:19). The doors were locked because the disciples were scared. The Roman soldiers were still on the prowl, and the crowds were still riled up from the Friday before.

However, no bolt or barricade could keep Jesus out. Jesus, risen from the dead, did, can, and will go everywhere and anywhere. There is no physical or earthly wall, barrier, or locked door that can keep Him from being near us.

That's good to keep in mind during these tough days. Those of you who can't visit family members in hospitals or nursing homes, Jesus can get there. Those in isolation or self-quarantine at home feel alone and are yearning for some company. Jesus can and does enter through your locked door. Those of you at home right now wondering if the Lord is with you like He is at our regular Sunday Masses, He is. No quarantine or locked door can keep Jesus out.

2. "He showed them His hands and His side" (John 20:20). The reason for doing so is clear: He wanted to convince the disciples that it was really He, the same one nailed to the cross, the same one whose side was opened with the spear by the Roman soldiers. I propose there's another reason why: our glorious risen Savior, the conqueror of sin, Satan, and eternal death, still has scars, and those scars led to His victory. You can only get to Easter Sunday through Good Friday, or as we're

more likely to say today, "No pain, no gain." This is called redemptive suffering. As it says in 1 Peter 1:6–7, "In this you rejoice, although now for a little while you may have to suffer through various trials, so that the genuineness of your faith, more precious than gold that is perishable even though tested by fire, may prove to be for praise, glory, and honor at the revelation of Jesus Christ."

About a week ago, I chatted at a safe distance with a man I met on a walk. He told me he'd recently recovered from the dreaded virus, and I rejoiced with him and thanked God for that. Then he said, "Look, here's the scab where they put the IV in my arm. And if you were closer, you'd see the lines on my face from the oxygen attachments." He showed me his wounds.

With so many lives disrupted and so many people suffering today, we may be tempted to wonder if the Lord knows what we're going through. When you question God, think again, and let Him show you His wounds.

3. "My Lord and my God" (John 20:28). These five small words, spoken by "doubting Thomas," are a moving expression of humble faith. Thomas had not been there Easter Sunday night when Jesus

miraculously showed up through the locked doors to the other apostles. He refused to believe that Jesus had really risen from the dead until he had hard, clinical evidence. Sure enough, the following Sunday, Thomas doubted no longer, falling to his hands and knees in awe as Jesus returned.

Thomas doesn't get into a long-winded, lengthy explanation. Instead, overawed by God's power and amazed at the Lord's ability to bring life from death and good from evil, he falls to his knees and utters five words: "My Lord and my God." We can do the same.

On this Divine Mercy Sunday, we would also do well to remember five other words: "Jesus, I trust in you." These words are a beautiful act of faith. Remember, there are no locked doors where Jesus is concerned. He bears His wounds still, and so do we. When it's hard to figure out or to find reason in what's going on today, we can't go wrong in praying, "My Lord and My God! Jesus, I trust in you!"

Sunday Mass, April 19, 2020

READINGS FOR REFLECTION:
Acts of the Apostles 2:42–47; Psalm 118:2–4, 13–15, 22–24;
1 Peter 1:3–9; John 20:19–31

CHAPTER 14

Faith *and* Reason

"Amen, amen, I say to you,
unless one is born of water and Spirit
he cannot enter the Kingdom of God.
What is born of flesh is flesh
and what is born of spirit is spirit."

—John 3:5–6

On the news recently, I observed two points of view that seemed to clash. On the one hand, there was a political leader who was giving us the good news that the coronavirus might be letting up. He went on to praise, rightly so, the physicians, scientists, researchers, and other professionals who had given us safety precautions. Then he said that God had nothing to do with this; it was all due to the work of doctors, researchers, scientists, and leaders.

Then I saw a protest march against all the regulations, safety requirements, and stay-at-home orders. A truck had a big sign on it that said, "Jesus is my vaccination." Hmm. Which of those two sides would you come down on—faith or science?

You know who can help us with this debate? St. Anselm, whose feast we celebrate today. He lived in the eleventh century, but his insights still apply. A towering theologian, one of Anselm's greatest contributions is his insistence on the alliance between faith and reason. Faith and reason aren't in opposition, he tells us; instead, they work together in a grand choreography.

The greatest supernatural gift that God has given us is *faith*. The greatest natural gift He has given us is *reason*. It would be strange if those two gifts clashed. God intends them to work in harmony. That provides us an answer to the polar opposites I mentioned earlier.

To the leader who says that God has nothing to do with this, we say you get an A+ in reason but an F in faith. You're right that all the safety requirements we've instituted have worked well. But they came at the inspiration of God, who imparted that reason and gave those people the wisdom to achieve what they have.

And to the person driving the protest truck, we would say you get an A+ in faith but an F in reason. Yes, Jesus is the Divine Physician who will bring health and healing in all of this. But one way He does this is through scientists, physicians, vaccinations, and prudent safety and health requirements. St. Anselm would say that we need *both* faith and reason. If you have one without the other, you're going to be in trouble because you'll probably become a fanatic or fundamentalist on either side. We need both to have a God-driven, reasoned approach to life.

Tuesday Mass, April 21, 2020

READINGS FOR REFLECTION:
Acts of the Apostles 4:32–37; Psalm 93:1ab, 1cd–2, 5; John 3:7b–15

CHAPTER 15

The Church Is Never Closed

I will bless the LORD at all times;
his praise shall be ever in my mouth.
Let my soul glory in the LORD;
the lowly will hear me and be glad.

—Psalm 34:2–3

Is "the Church" closed for the virus?

No way! Fuhgeddaaboudit! Never in your life!

Now the church with a small *c* might be locked—although many are open for a good part of each day so that folks can pray—and the public celebration of the Mass is on hold for a while.

But the Church with a capital *C* can never be closed. The Church is not a building, but "living stones"—you and me, with the apostles as the foundation and Jesus as the cornerstone—and is more alive than ever.

No one, nowhere can close the Church. Oh, not that some haven't tried, when thugs in places like China, Nigeria, parts of India, and Syria are indeed trying not only to close the Church but exterminate it. History tells us that they're wasting their time. Ask Nero, the Barbarians, Napoleon, Hitler, or Stalin, just to name a few.

If these people had succeeded, well then, Jesus must have been a deceiver. He's the One who assured us that "the gates of hell shall not prevail" because "I will be with you for all ages, even until the end of the world." To even hint that Jesus fibbed is blasphemy, for He is "the Way, the Truth, and the Life."

Well, some skeptics continue, "The Mass and the sacraments are closed to us."

True, we miss regular Sunday Mass, Holy Communion, and Confession deeply, and long for their return. But Mass is offered daily by our priests, and no Eucharist is private. Every time we priests have the honor of approaching the altar, we are in the company of God—Father, Son, and Holy Spirit—our Blessed Mother, the Communion of Saints, and all of God's People, so that "from the rising of the sun to its setting, a pure sacrifice may be offered to your name."

Our parish priests have risen to the occasion with innovative ways to distribute Holy Communion, expose the Blessed Sacrament for adoration, hear Confessions, and anoint and visit the sick. They assemble at gravesides to bury our dead. Our courageous chaplains in hospitals and nursing homes are on the front lines with the fortification of the sacraments. All this is accomplished with care given to protection, sanitation, and distancing, as we have a moral obligation never to compromise our own health or that of others.

Then there is the crescendo of prayer sounding in the hearts of families and folks by themselves who are united with Jesus and His Church in the sanctuary of their baptized souls. Many are telling us that their prayer, their reliance on the Bible, their consciousness of the spiritual connection we have in the Body of Christ, the Church, are more alive than ever.

Don't forget the faith that keeps our healthcare professionals going, the hope that animates our essential workers as they know they're helping us all, the charity that inspires so many neighbors, community volunteers, and employees to work even more generously.

The Church's healthcare apostolate—in these acres of the Lord's vast vineyard called the Archdiocese of New York, found in ArchCare and in the many hospitals, health facilities, visiting professionals, and nursing homes often cared for by sisters—hums along with an even more accelerated energy. Catholic Charities is serving more meals than ever, keeping an eye out for those scared and forgotten, such as immigrants and refugees, and providing our parishes with sustenance to assist their struggling people.

Our religious education engine is purring, with classes, catechesis, faith formation, reflections, and Bible study up and running online.

Our acclaimed Catholic schools are in session, with dedicated teachers instructing their students at a distance and counting on parents to exercise their duty as the "primary educators."

Our parish priests have become creative in using technology to keep in touch with their people, especially the homebound, and to provide virtual Masses and devotions.

Can any of us deny that the radiance of the Lord's Resurrection is obvious in the sense of unity and purpose that we detect in the leadership of our civic leaders and medical professionals and in the rediscovered, deep-down longing for God that the frustration, helplessness, and adversity of this virus has uncovered?

Don't give me any of that "the Church is closed" nonsense! "The Church's one foundation is Jesus Christ her Lord," and He is for sure not on sabbatical!

As Pope St. John Paul II often exhorted, "Love for Jesus and His Church is the passion of our lives."

And as Pope Francis told me when he telephoned recently, "Tell your people their faith, hope, and love inspire us all."

The Church is open!

Wednesday Column, April 22, 2020

READINGS FOR REFLECTION:

Acts of the Apostles 5:17–26; Psalm 34:2–3, 4–5, 6–7, 8–9; John 3:16–21

CHAPTER 16

And They Recognized Him

That very day, the first day of the week,
two of Jesus' disciples were going
to a village seven miles from Jerusalem called Emmaus,
and they were conversing about all the things that
had occurred.

—Luke 24:13–14

"The Road to Emmaus" is the title of this epic Gospel from Luke, handed down through the ages. It's one of the richest and most enlightening episodes that we have. What is Jesus teaching us in this renowned passage? Let me concentrate on four points.

1. "But their eyes were prevented from recognizing him" (Luke 24:16). It is Easter Sunday, and two of Jesus' disciples are walking away from Jerusalem to Emmaus, a village about seven miles away. And who comes along to walk with them but Jesus,

risen from the dead. But the disciples' eyes were prevented from recognizing Him.

How could that be? Why didn't they recognize Jesus? Well, logically speaking, He was probably the last person they expected to see. After all, He had been crucified. He was dead and buried. Some speculate that Jesus had been transformed by His Resurrection and that's why they didn't recognize Him. But let me propose another more classical interpretation: the disciples were so wrapped up in their own worries about the events of the Friday before that they didn't even look that closely at Him. The Gospel even tells us they were looking downcast (Luke 24:17), literally, looking down.

What is Jesus teaching us here? Don't look down to the ground. Where does the Lord want us to look? He wants us to look deep within, where there is meaning and purpose; to look around at people who love us, help us, and care for us. He wants us to look up at Him, at the One who never abandons but walks with us. The Lord wants us to feel sorry for others in distress, He wants us to feel sorry for our sins, but He does not want us to feel sorry for ourselves, like those two downcast disciples.

2. Jesus asks them, "Was it not necessary that the Messiah should suffer these things and enter into his glory?" (Luke 24:26). Jesus had to suffer and die so He could rise, as there is no Easter Sunday without Good Friday. So, don't fall for the temptation that suffering is a sign that the Lord is *not* with us. In fact, it is a sign that, indeed, He is! We can bear anything, philosophers, psychologists, and spiritual writers tell us, if we know there is a reason and a purpose, even if it is not clear at the moment. Through His adversity, Jesus rose to new life. So do we.

3. When did the two disciples figure out who He was? The two disciples stopped at an inn on the road for a meal, and they invited their still-unrecognized companion to eat with them. "And it happened that, while he was with them at table, he took bread, said the blessing, broke it, and gave it to them. With that their eyes were opened and they recognized Him" (Luke 24:30–31). Jesus repeated what He had done the night before He died, at the Last Supper on that first Holy Thursday. And then their eyes were opened—it's He! They recognized Him in the

Eucharist at Mass. And with that, He vanished from their sight.

No wonder we miss Mass and Holy Communion so much these days—that's where He is still powerfully with us. As Dorothy Day wrote, "Without the sacraments of the Church, especially the Eucharist, I couldn't go on."

4. What did our two slow learners do? They returned to Jerusalem. It dawned on them that they had been going the wrong way. They were running away from Jerusalem but would now return. Maybe this dreaded virus is an invitation from the Lord for us to change course. Is it time for us, as a Church, as families, as a nation, to "return to Jerusalem"? I hear it all the time, in phone calls, letters, people I wave at on the street, commentators, journalists. They say the pandemic has shaken them up, and their faith is coming back. They realized that they've been looking for meaning in a lot of dead ends; maybe they've put a career before family or let social media or something else become their idols. But now it's time to "return to Jerusalem," to our faith in God, and in the Church.

In 1992, I had the privilege of going on a three-week pilgrimage to the Holy Land. The day before we were to depart to head back to the States was a free day, and I told our Franciscan guide that there was one place I wanted to visit. "Where's that?" Fr. Godfrey asked me. "Emmaus," I said. "I want to go to Emmaus. And I want to walk those seven miles that St. Luke speaks about."

Fr. Godfrey paused and said, "Afraid you can't." I asked why. He said, "No one knows where that village of Emmaus really was." Fr. Godfrey could see that I was disappointed. He said to me, "Ah, but there's the wisdom, dear Timothy. Don't be discouraged. Jesus intends that every road you take, every journey you embark upon, every walk you begin is in fact the road to Emmaus. And He walks along with you."

Sunday Mass, April 26, 2020

READINGS FOR REFLECTION:
Acts of the Apostles 2:14, 22–33; Psalm 16:1–2, 5, 7–8, 9–10, 11;
1 Peter 1:17–21; Luke 24:13–35

CHAPTER 17

Good and Evil

Those who had been scattered by the persecution
that arose because of Stephen
went as far as Phoenicia, Cyprus, and Antioch,
preaching the word to no one but Jews.

—Acts of the Apostles 11:19

Our faith tells us that God does not cause evil, but He can bring good out of evil. We have an example of that in chapter 11 of the Acts of the Apostles.

The early Church faced terrible persecution in Jerusalem. Many of the first-generation members of the Church understandably fled the city and went to Damascus and Antioch, among other places, and spread the faith through preaching and service. Because of them, more and more people began to believe in Jesus Christ and express the desire to be incorporated into Him in and through His Church.

The evil of the persecution brought about good, as more people, seeing the examples of these followers of Jesus, began to enter the Church. This included people who were not Jewish. As the Good News spread, more Gentiles started to follow the ways of Jesus. Eventually, after much controversy and argument, the decision was made that the invitation of Jesus was intended for everybody.

So, you see how God can bring good out of evil. That's important to remember these days as we are all burdened with the evil of the coronavirus. We could begin to ask ourselves what graces, good, and growth can come from this evil.

Tuesday Mass, May 5, 2020

READINGS FOR REFLECTION:
Acts of the Apostles 11:19–26; Psalm 87:1b–3, 4–5, 6–7;
John 10:22–30

CHAPTER 18

Words and Deeds

Always be ready to give an explanation
to anyone who asks you for a reason for your hope,
but do it with gentleness and reverence.

—1 Peter 3:15–16

In the first letter of St. Peter, the apostle addressed those first-generation Christians who were persecuted and even martyred for the faith. But he also addresses us in that letter, compelling you and me to present and defend our faith. It is our great duty.

I think of the great saints and geniuses of the past who have defended the faith, such as the apostles, St. Paul, St. Augustine, and St. Thomas Aquinas. More recently, I think of St. Teresa Benedicta of the Cross, Archbishop Fulton Sheen, Cardinal Avery Dulles, and Bishop Robert Barron. We call these eloquent speakers and writers "apologists." Apologetics is the art of being able to present the truths of our faith in a credible and compelling way. The folks I've mentioned have done this with particular flair and effectiveness. But St. Peter's point, both back then and now, was that each of us is charged with that very thing—to always be ready to give an explanation to anyone who asks a reason for our hope.

We do this by word and by example, by the way we live and conduct ourselves. Pope St. Paul VI reminds us that people are moved more by witness than by words. That's not new, of course. We see that in the Acts of the Apostles: "The crowds paid attention to what was said by Philip when they heard it and saw the signs he was doing" (8:6). Words and witness. Words and deeds.

We know that this change of heart happened often in the early Church. In the era of persecution, as tens of thousands cheered the lions mauling the Christians, there were hundreds who were whispering in the silence of their hearts, *What is it about these so-called Christians that would inspire them to be faithful even under such trials?* The persecutions of the Christians became like gray hairs: when we pull one out, ten new ones come back in their place. The more Christians in the early days of the faith were persecuted, the more other people were attracted to Jesus and His Church.

Tertullian, an early apologist, would write, "The blood of the martyrs is the seed of the faith."

So, a question for all of us is whether we are ready to give an explanation to anyone who asks a reason for our hope. A lot of people need a reason for hope these days. To a society tempted to believe there is no God, to those people who call believers superstitious, naïve, or illiterate, we say no. We believe in the One who revealed, "I am the Lord, Thy God. Thou shalt not have strange gods before me."

To a culture that Pope Francis calls "throwaway," which posits that all human life—from the baby in the womb, to the abandoned immigrant, to a dying grandma, to a prisoner on death row—can be discarded and destroyed, we say *No!* We believe that all human life, from conception to natural death, is sacred and inviolable.

To a system that believes that money is the most important thing, we say by our words and actions that when money becomes a god, money becomes the devil.

To a mindset that holds that sexual pleasure is our entitlement, we propose in our marriages and families that sexual love is a reflection of God's love for us, intended by God only for a man and woman united in the lifelong, life-giving, faithful love of marriage.

And today, when a city, a nation, and a planet finds itself wearied and wiped out by some strange plague of biblical proportions and asks how we can hope any longer, we, as the Church, listen to the One who called Himself the Way, the Truth, and the Life (John 14:6).

These reasons for hope are offered not just in words but by witness in action. St. Peter said, "Do it with gentleness and reverence, keeping your consciences clear" (1 Peter 3:16). The current successor of St. Peter, Pope Francis, urges us to win people over with joy and love. And as the Holy Father's own patron saint, St. Francis of Assisi, recommended, "Preach at all times. Use words only when necessary."

Sunday Mass, May 17, 2020

READINGS FOR REFLECTION:
Acts of the Apostles 8:5–8, 14–17; Psalm 66:1–3, 4–5, 6–7, 16, 20;
1 Peter 3:15–18; John 14:15–21

CHAPTER 19

Final Perseverance

Jesus said to his disciples:
"When the Advocate comes
whom I will send you from the Father,
the Spirit of truth that proceeds from the Father,
he will testify to me."

—John 15:26

Jesus spoke these words to His closest friends: "I have told you this so that you may not fall away" (John 16:1).

Jesus knows how difficult it is to follow His teachings. He knows that we will meet with opposition, disdain, harassment, persecution, and even martyrdom. So, He recognizes that we will all face the temptation to fall away.

In the midst of this pandemic, I've worried that the trauma of the coronavirus would tempt people to lose their faith, but I'm happy to see that the opposite is

I AM WITH YOU

the case. Recent evidence shows that people's faith has been strengthened.

A crisis can do that, right? It can strengthen our faith or weaken it.

Jesus warns us that we should be on guard not to let our faith weaken in times of adversity. The tougher things get, the more our faith is needed.

There's a beautiful tradition called the "final perseverance," where we pray that when our hour comes and death is near, our faith in Jesus will be strong and durable to get us through.

We even say that in the Hail Mary: ". . . now and at the hour of our death."

Be strong in Christ.

Monday Mass, May 18, 2020

READINGS FOR REFLECTION:
Acts of the Apostles 16:11–15; Psalm 149:1b–2, 3–4, 5–6a 9b;
John 15:26—16:4a

Chapter 20

Refuge

Lord, you have been our refuge through all generations.

—Psalm 90:1

We are tempted to believe that the turmoil and trauma, the sufferings and challenges of the day in which we live, are unprecedented. Of course, our elders will remind us of the difficulties they endured in the past. Human history is filled with difficulties; our own personal history is filled with them.

When we're tempted to despair, we need to remember that we've been through it before. And so, we say, "Lord, you have been our refuge through all generations."

Tuesday Mass, June 2, 2020

READINGS FOR REFLECTION:
2 Peter 3:12–15a, 17–18; Psalm 90:2, 3–4, 10, 14, 16;
Ephesians 1:17–18; Mark 12:13–17

CHAPTER 21

God Is in All of This

"As the LORD lives, and as you yourself live,
I will not leave you," Elisha replied.

—2 Kings 2:2

We will be talking about COVID-19 for a long time. Our kids and grandkids will ask us about it. The pandemic isn't over yet, I realize. But it's not too premature to ponder what we've learned from these trying months. Here are a few lessons I've gleaned:

1. The Lord has been with us. So many tell me, "My prayer has been more frequent and fruitful. Just as I was questioning where God was in all this, I discovered that He's right here."

2. We miss the Mass and the sacraments. A faith made more durable by trial has made us long for Holy Communion, Confession, Baptism, Confirmation, Matrimony, and the Anointing of

the Sick. Thank God the sacraments are on the way back!

3. We need one another. Being quarantined and isolated has left us thirsty for the company of family and friends. Not to be able to comfort and embrace the sick and the fragile has wounded us. Community is essential for us.

4. People are good. What a boost to see our healthcare workers, police, first responders, essential workers, sanitation laborers, and yes, even our political leaders, so devoted and energetic.

5. Routine is not all that bad. Most of the time we dread Mondays and groan at going back to work or to school. Not anymore. We've learned the effectiveness of a routine, of a scheduled, responsible life. Spending all day in pajamas is good for an occasional snow day, but not for months on end. Let's pray for a more focused and aware routine now and in the future.

6. Nurturing the mind and soul is a necessity. Reading, praying, reflecting, studying—we classically call this the "interior life"—is a significant ingredient in the recipe for a healthy, wholesome, and holy life.

7. An ordered day, with set goals, is an antidote to boredom and bad habits. How many people are reporting, "At first I slept in every morning and channel-surfed most of the day. Then it dawned on me that this was toxic." Get up! Get dressed! Set some goals and a schedule for the day! Go to bed at night with a sense of accomplishment.

8. Too much news is counterproductive. Yes, reliable newscasters are helpful in providing crucial information and keeping us together. But listening and watching know-it-alls give their opinions all day is bad for your mind and soul. Turn the TV off and pray, read the Bible, or talk with family members, loved ones, and friends.

9. "Fear is useless." Jesus said that, by the way. Can't we all recall fretting over an occasional cough and fatigue, nervous that we were the newest victim of the virus? It got us nowhere. ". . . What is needed is trust!" goes the rest of that quote from the Gospel.

10. The safety and well-being of others are as important as my own, and more important than my convenience, comfort, and selfish desires. That's termed "the common good," and, as far back as Aristotle and Plato, the protection of the

common good was considered a necessity for a civilized, enlightened society. Pope St. John Paul II called it solidarity. We're in this together; we look out and care for one another, especially the weak and fragile. I'm so proud of the human family for putting the common good first these past three months. The crisis will, please God, abate; our concern for the common good cannot.

11. We're rather good company to ourselves. The philosopher Blaise Pascal remarked, "All our problems boil down to our inability to be happy in our room by ourselves." Silence—with no distractions; no ability to buy, spend, or talk—isn't too bad if we learn to be at peace with ourselves. To be sure, too much of it can drive us nuts, but it's a talent to be cultivated.

Each time I make my annual retreat, I recall the counsel of a director when I was a young priest: "Look back and sense where God was in all this."

Not bad advice as normalcy slowly returns.

Thursday Column, June 18, 2020

READINGS FOR REFLECTION:
2 Kings 2:1, 6–14; Psalm 31:20, 21, 24; Matthew 6:1–6, 16–18

CHAPTER 22

J-O-Y

"I give praise to you, Father, Lord of heaven and earth,
for although you have hidden these things
from the wise and the learned
you have revealed them to the childlike."

—Matthew 11:25

In the last chapter, I shared with you some wisdom I had picked up over the first three months of quarantine. That exercise prompted me to reflect even more, and additional thoughts came to mind:

1. We are not ultimately in charge. OK, true enough, our initiative and responsibility are essential, but certain things are beyond our domain. We usually attribute an omniscience to scientists, scholars, and physicians. Through this crisis, we admired their skills and hard work, but we often saw them shrug and admit, "I don't know." Even our

political leaders, who enjoy appearing to have all the answers, often concluded, "I'm baffled. I don't know where this is going to go."

2. We are not God. That moving act of faith, "Jesus, I trust in Thee!" so frequently found itself on my lips over the course of the pandemic. My dad used to say, "You can't do anything about the weather; you can't do much when you're stuck in traffic—those are good reminders that we can't control everything." Add COVID-19 to weather and traffic.

3. Simple is better. I read an article about how moms, dads, and kids had grown closer during the lockdown. (Not to deny there was tension as well.) No complicated plans or detailed projects. We're talking about reading a book to the kids, playing a board game, writing notes together to Grandma and Grandpa, baking cookies and leaving a tray outside the elderly neighbor's door.

One dad confessed that he spent hours on the floor each day coloring pictures with the kids. The food was simpler, too; I'm told grilled cheese for supper, pancakes for breakfast. Each member of the family pitched in. No elaborate wardrobes were needed, either. We couldn't even go to the barber or hair salon. All the complicated stuff that usually clutters our lives was gone, and we rather enjoyed it. Simplicity of life, a virtue extolled in the Bible, was the four-month blue-plate special.

4. We work to live, not live to work. "As I look back," a woman told me on the phone, "it's clear that, before COVID-19, home, even my husband and kids, were 'part time.' My real duty and drive in life was the job: ten to twelve hours a day, including some hours on Saturday and Sunday, with home just a 'flophouse' and the family an afterthought." "I've done a 180," she went on. "My life is not my job, or my profession, as much as I love it. Work is a *means* to an *end*, not the *end* itself; the *end* is my home, family, friends, and faith!" Alleluia! The Lord's been trying to remind us of that since the Garden of Eden.

5. Distance is not as effective as being there. Bravo to our priests who kept in touch effectively through live-streaming, email, Facebook, Twitter, phone, and walking the neighborhood to wave at the folks. As good as it was, and as welcome as it was in the pandemic, everybody concluded, "But it's just not the same."

A seasoned priest remarked, "We learned in the seminary that you can't have Mass without bread and wine. Now I've learned you can't have Mass without the people." He was quick to admit that, of course, Mass without a congregation was valid and a high good, but even such a Mass as that was never private because our faith tells us all of heaven and earth worship at every Eucharist.

So, we've had "distance" events. Good, but not the same. When I would gather around the open grave with a small group of family and friends, we yearned to embrace and offer condolences, but we couldn't.

Mom tells me, "Shannon and Chris brought little Mollie Rose by (her three-month-old great-grandchild), and I was so thrilled to see her. But I wanted to hug her and hold her on my lap. I could only coo at her from ten feet away."

We're meant to hold, touch, embrace, and be close. Distancing is okay in a pinch, but ultimately just doesn't do it.

Finally, as toxic as the virus is, the malady of feeling sorry for ourselves is far more so. Some of us moved into "pity city," which is usually the most crowded urban area on the planet.

6. St. Teresa of Calcutta taught that, if you want *joy*, spell out the word: "J" comes first, and is for *Jesus:* put Him first; "o" follows, and indicates *others*, as the needs of those around us take precedence; finally, arrives "y," for *yourself.* Put yourself last and be surprised by joy.

I reckon that, in spite of their weariness, emotional wounds, and some shock, our healthcare professionals are people of *joy* these days, relieved not only because the worst seems over, but because they served others so sacrificially rather than feeling sorry for themselves.

"Cursed the day that doesn't teach us something," goes the old saying.

The last hundred have certainly taught us a lot.

Thursday Column, July 16, 2020

READINGS FOR REFLECTION:
Isaiah 10:5–7, 13b–16; Psalm 94:5–6, 7–8, 9–10, 14–15;
Matthew 11:25–27

CHAPTER 23

The Church Will Survive

"I am with you always, until the end of the age."
—Matthew 28:20

Is the one, holy, catholic, and apostolic Church going to survive?

That's a question many people, both inside and outside Mother Church, are posing.

A couple of days ago, I was enjoying one of my favorite pastimes: a breakfast of eggs, sausage, and pancakes at a local diner.

Next to me was a table of three men, chatting over their corned beef hash and biscuits, unaware that I was eavesdropping.

"No way it can survive," observed one of the diners. "Folks have lost interest, the long suspension of activity made people shrug and figure they could get along without it, nobody's interested in going back once everything reopens, figuring they can watch all the stuff at home, and we're all tired of the scandals and money-asking."

Well, I grimaced, uncharacteristically losing my appetite. They obviously have answered the question "Will the Church survive?" with a big *no*.

There was a brief silence. Then the fellas picked up the conversation, as one commented, "And it's a shame the sport isn't going to make it because the Yankees and Aaron Judge are off to such a sizzling start!"

I rediscovered my appetite. They weren't talking about the Church at all, but about baseball!

Well, fact is, a lot of people are saying about the Church what those three were saying about baseball. It's not coming back.

My friends, it's time for a deep breath and an act of faith. To ask, "Will the Church survive?" is an oxymoron. We have God's Word, the most reliable guarantee there is, that the Church will indeed survive! Our Lord and Savior, the second Person of the Most Blessed Trinity, gave us this promise: "I am with you always, even until the end of the world. And not even the gates of hell can prevail against my Church."

Unlike baseball, the Church is not a human proposition. That human element is mighty important. That's where the saints are found, where we sinners are found. But the Church has a divine composition that assures us of her survival.

"The gates of hell shall not prevail against it," Jesus promises us. But as a confessor once reminded me, "That does not mean that hell will ever stop trying."

So we've got the sorrow and shackles of COVID-19; declining church attendance and donations; new allegations of sexual abuse from decades ago every day from tort attorneys, one of whom chants that he will "bring down the Church!"; closing of schools, merging of parishes; kids and grandkids not practicing their faith; not enough priests, deacons, religious sisters and brothers; folks arguing about Church teaching, whether Pope Francis is "too liberal" or "not liberal enough"; threats to religious freedom and the Church's liberty to teach and serve . . . oh dear. The "gates of hell" are at it full time.

While we can never conclude that the Church will not survive, we can wonder, "How?" What invitations from Jesus can we hear in all this turmoil? What is He asking from us, the faithful, weary members of His Church?

An old Latin phrase applies: *Ecclesia semper reformanda*—The Church is always in need of reform.

Reform for her people, her leaders—I sure need it—her structures, her pastoral strategy.

Jesus, of course, bids us not to tread water, but to "cast out to the deep!" While the essentials of the Church, as given to us by the Lord, cannot change, the way we live them, pass them on, and apply them sure can.

In every shout of a crisis we detect a whispered invitation from the Lord to reform and renewal.

Last week, I visited a wonderful group of religious women, the Franciscan Sisters of the Renewal. Next to their convent in Harlem, where they live in community, form their novices, and serve the poor, was a crumbling, unused church. Last year they asked me if they could clean it up and use it for their community prayers.

"Be my guest," I gratefully replied.

That's where we welcomed four new novices on the Feast of Our Lady of the Angels. And the church—freshly painted, repaired with a new roof and floor in the sanctuary—sparkled!

The reading at the liturgy for the novices recounted St. Francis doing the same thing in Assisi: repairing and renewing the crumbling church dedicated to Our Lady.

That's our charge, our dream, our dare: to rebuild, renew, and restore His Church.

Because, make no doubt about it, the Church will survive! We members couldn't destroy it if we tried—and tried we have.

(By the way, I'm confident that baseball will survive too.)

Thursday Column, August 13, 2020

READINGS FOR REFLECTION:
Ezekiel 9:1–7; 10:18–22; Psalm 113:1–2, 3–4, 5–6; Matthew 18:15–20

Afterword by Kathryn Jean Lopez

"The worst oppression is a life without God."

It was Easter Sunday 2020, and Cardinal Dolan was quoting Russian novelist and political prisoner Alexander Solzhenitsyn during his morning homily. I was feeling the truth of these words in my bones because I was experiencing a life without God. Many of us were having similar experiences. With churches closed around the country, every inch of me wanted to be present for the Holy Sacrifice of the Mass. My longing for the sacraments—especially the Eucharist—was real and insatiable.

Honestly, I was drowning a bit in my sadness. I cried a lot during those coronavirus days, especially during Lent and Easter. In many ways, Lent never seemed to end. I've since talked to others who shared that they felt abandoned by the Church during the pandemic. Others I've spoken to have left the Church and don't plan on coming back. If my own personal distress wasn't enough, I lament this sense of loss that so many others have experienced.

I can understand where some of these people are coming from. The virtual is a poor substitute for the Real Presence, but via YouTube from St. Patrick's on Easter Sunday, Cardinal Dolan helped ease some of the pain I was experiencing. Christ hadn't abandoned me; my pastor friend was helping me see this truth. He was walking with me in sadness, with a similar longing to see people in churches again.

Granted, unlike me, Cardinal Dolan was present for the Mass, but he was experiencing his own Passion in not being able to minister in the ways we are accustomed. Maybe he was preaching to himself as he was pulling me out of darkness when he said, "Emptiness can be a blessing, not a curse. It is the God of the living who fills us with meaning, resolve, light, and hope. He has risen as He said He would. *Alleluia, Alleluia*."

To this day, those words pull me out of myself, away from the distractions of the world—politics, social media, our daily obligations—right back to Jesus. These distractions can draw us away from God in ways we aren't even aware of.

I remember being with Cardinal Dolan in Rome for the canonization of Popes John XXIII and John Paul II and listening to Pope Francis talking about the wounds of Christ. Both popes knew our human need for true knowledge of those glorified wounds. As Cardinal Dolan puts it, "Our glorious risen Savior, the conqueror of sin, Satan, and eternal death, still has wounds. As a matter of fact, and this is what He wanted to demonstrate, those scars led to His victory."

You don't need Cardinal Dolan or anyone else to tell you about the miseries of the world. They surround us. They are within us. This coronavirus experience—as grave, painful, confusing, and deadening as it has been—is something of God's mercy, too. Even to this day, as we bemoan the strife in the world and on our streets, in our families and in our hearts, Cardinal Dolan brings us back to our faith: "Jesus, I trust in you." This isn't just a pious utterance; it is the prayer for our lives from the depths of our hearts. This is the challenge: do we or don't we trust in Him? It's a journey, and it has to be all-encompassing. We don't trust Him in one thing and not another. That's not the Christian life. So, we begin again and pray with all the conviction we can muster, "Jesus, help me trust in you. In everything. Always."

When we can truly pray, "Jesus, I trust in you," graces flow from merely wanting to trust. As Cardinal Dolan says in this powerful book you have just read, "This is a beautiful act of faith similar to that of doubting Thomas. . . . [R]emember there are no locked doors where Jesus is concerned. He bears His wounds still, and so do we. When it's hard to figure out or find reason in what's going on today, we can't go wrong in praying: 'My Lord and my God! Jesus, I trust in you!'"

There is no full return to normal after the coronavirus. At least there shouldn't be. We need to be transformed so that we are truly living our lives as beacons of the people of hope that we are called to be in the world. Pray that through this experience we've endured, we are transformed into the Christians we are called to be, people infused with the Holy Spirit and filled with love for and of the Trinity.

The world needs us to be authentic, bold, and loving in the ways of Jesus Christ. Now is the time for us to set the world aflame with humble yet confident authenticity in our faith. It's the only time we have. I can't say this enough: we need to pray for one another and encourage one another. I've been encouraged and challenged by the words in this book in the most important of ways, and I pray that you have been, too.

Kathryn Jean Lopez, Senior Fellow,
National Review Institute
and author of *A Year with the Mystics*
The Nativity of the Blessed Virgin Mary,
September 8, 2020

Acknowledgments

A big thank you to Joseph Zwilling, Lino Rulli, and Gary Jansen for their encouragement and support in bringing this book to light.

I also want to to express my gratitude to *Catholic New York* for allowing me to reprint some of my weekly columns in this book.

About the Author

His Eminence Cardinal Timothy M. Dolan was named Archbishop of New York by Pope Benedict XVI in 2009. Previously, he served as the tenth Archbishop of Milwaukee after being named by Pope John Paul II in 2002. Cardinal Dolan is the author of several books, including *Called to Be Holy*, *Doers of the Word*, and the national best seller *Who Do You Say I Am?*